MOON WHEELS

Ruth Fainlight was born in New York City, and has lived mostly in England since the age of 15. Her father was born in London, and her mother in a small town on the eastern borders of the Austro-Hungarian Empire (now in Ukraine). She was educated at schools in America and England, and at Birmingham and Brighton colleges of art, and married the writer Alan Sillitoe in 1959. She was Poet in Residence at Vanderbilt University, Nashville, Tennessee, in 1985 and 1990, and received a Cholmondeley Award for Poetry in 1994.

Her many books include poetry, short stories, translations, drama and opera libretti. Her poems have appeared in numerous anthologies, and her stories in books including *The Penguin Book of Modern Women's Stories* (1991), *Caught in a Story: contemporary fairy-tales and fables* (Vintage, 1992), *Contemporary Jewish Writing* (University of Nebraska Press, 1998) and *The Penguin Book of the Beach* (2001).

Her poetry books include: *Cages* (1966) and *To See the Matter Clearly* (1968), from Macmillan in Britain and Dufour in the USA; *The Region's Violence* (1973), *Another Full Moon* (1976), *Sibyls and Others* (1980), *Fifteen to Infinity* (1983), *Selected Poems* (1987) and *The Knot* (1990), all from Hutchinson and Century Hutchinson; *This Time of Year* (1994) and *Selected Poems* (1995) from Sinclair-Stevenson; and *Climates* (1983), *Sugar-Paper Blue* (1997), *Burning Wire* (2002) and *Moon Wheels* (2006) from Bloodaxe Books. *Fifteen to Infinity* was published in the USA by Carnegie Mellon University Press. *Sugar-Paper Blue* was shortlisted for the Whitbread Poetry Award.

She has also translated two books of poetry from the Portuguese of Sophia de Mello Breyner, and collaborated with Alan Sillitoe on *All Citizens Are Soldiers*, a translation of Lope de Vega's play *Fuenteovejuna*. Her own poetry has been published in Portuguese (1995), French (1997), Spanish (2000 & 2005) and Italian (2003) editions.

She has published two collections of short stories, *Daylife and Nightlife* (André Deutsch, 1971) and *Dr Clock's Last Case* (Virago, 1994). Her libretti include: *The Dancer Hotoke* (1991), a chamber opera by Erika Fox (nominated for the Laurence Oliver Awards in 1992); *The European Story* (1993), a chamber opera by Geoffrey Alvarez; and *Bedlam Britannica* (1995), a Channel Four *War Cries* TV opera directed by Celia Lowenstein with music by Robert Jan Stips.

RUTH FAINLIGHT

Moon Wheels

BLOODAXE BOOKS

ISBN: 1 85224 742 8

First published 2006 by
Bloodaxe Books Ltd,
Highgreen,
Tarset,
Northumberland NE48 1RP.

www.bloodaxebooks.com
For further information about Bloodaxe titles
please visit our website or write to
the above address for a catalogue.

Bloodaxe Books Ltd acknowledges
the financial assistance of
Arts Council England, North East.

Cover printing by J. Thomson Colour Printers Ltd, Glasgow.

Printed in Great Britain by
Bell & Bain Limited, Glasgow, Scotland.

for Alan

ACKNOWLEDGEMENTS

Acknowledgements are due to the editors of the following pub-
lications where some of the new poems – sometimes in dif-
ferent versions – first appeared: *Acumen, Ars Interpres, Eight,
London Magazine, Manhattan Review, Modern Poetry in Trans-
lation, Painted, spoken, Poetry London, PN Review, Poetry
Review* and *Threepenny Review*.

'A Lost Painting by Balthus' was first published in *The
Great Cat: Poems about Cats*, ed. Emily Fragos (Everyman's
Library, 2005). 'The Garden of Eden' and 'War Moon' were
first published in *100 Poets Against the War*, ed. Todd Swift
(Salt, 2003).

The poems reprinted from *This Time of Year* (Sinclair-
Stevenson, 1994) first appeared in *The Charlston Magazine,
Critical Quarterly, The Duncan Lawrie Journal, The London
Review of Books, The New Yorker, The Observer, The Poetry
Book Society Anthology 2*, ed. Anne Stevenson (Poetry Book
Society/Hutchinson, 1991), *Poetry Durham, Southwest Review,
The Spectator* and *The Times Literary Supplement*.

The eight poems from *Twelve Sibyls* were first published
by Gehenna Press (USA) in 1991 in *Twelve Sibyls*, with wood-
cuts by Leonard Baskin, and reprinted in *This Time of Year*.

The poems by Sophia de Mello Breyner were first pub-
lished in *Marine Rose* (Black Swan Books, USA, 1987).

'Jocasta's Death' is from a new translation of Sophocles'
Theban Plays by Ruth Fainlight & Robert Littman, to be
published by Johns Hopkins University Press.

An earlier version of 'A Postcard from Tunisia' is the text
for an artist book with prints by Judith Rothchild, pub-
lished in 2004 by Éditions Verdigris, France.

Seven of the new poems and nine from *This Time of Year*
were published with Spanish translations in *Diario de Poesía*
(Buenos Aires) in 2006.

CONTENTS

II Translations

III Poems from *This Time of Year*

IV Eight Poems from *Twelve Sibyls*

NEW POEMS

Apogee

A silent wary cat, prowling the hall
end to end, in the blanched light that pours
through uncurtained windows and open door
a glaze of silver hoar-frost across the floor,
in tune with traffic-murmur and aircraft-roar
I tread soft, to mute the creaking boards.

Alert and feverish in the cloudy dawn
of the first chill autumn night before
the exact apogee of its orbit
between wax and wane – as the moon alters
course and turns its high, hard, wide, bald
brow toward the dark, I wait for morning.

Moon Wheels

The sky is clear and dark, the moon's disk
far away and small and silver-bright.
Its cold beam probes through my window:
the torch of a seeker, invisible
behind a cone of wavering light.

Too much on my mind to let me sleep.
A disk of rubbish, half-submerged
in foamy surf, swirls through pier-struts.
Then I remember: full moon tonight.
I cannot hide from this disturbing muse.

We lurch together, drunken lovers:
two sides of a coin which can never
see each other – sky-disk, world-rubbish –
one sharply incised as if new-minted,
the opposite worn smooth, illegible,

or two wheels which cannot stop grinding
between them the coarse stuff
of existence, images and words,
into a substance called poetry. The process
is indescribable. And its purpose.

Moving

Sit down among the boxes and write a poem,
he told me; obedient, I'm writing.
Moving house, he said, is such an ordinary
thing to do – a regular activity,
especially for you – no obligation
to unpack at once or be too dutiful.

Find a vacant corner and there among
half-empty cartons spilling crumpled paper,
piles of sofa cushions and rolled-up carpets,
dining chairs like acrobatic couples
or swimmers, chest to chest, one pair of legs
trailing through water, the other flailing air,

and think about important things – not builders,
plumbers, electricians. I try to remember
how it began, this restlessness: a lifetime
trying to feel at home. A need and hope, he
hints, which might be programmed in my genes,
bred in the bone – nothing to do with him –

and makes me realise again those complex
ties that hold us together: everywhere,
both of us are strangers. Then: 'Let's open
a bottle of wine and drink a toast to life,'
he smiles and holds me close, 'then go upstairs.'
Why not? I ponder, putting the poem aside.

Blankets

The stuffy ground-floor bedroom
at the back of our flat. The bed,
covered with blue Witney blankets
bound with paler blue velvet.

Measles, scarlet fever,
influenza, whooping cough.
The night I tripped over the oil-stove
Mother lit to warm the bathroom.

From hip to heel, burning
paraffin splashed. Weeks in bed
under a sort of cradle made
to hold the weight of the blankets off.

Bunches of flowers, orange and red,
climbed the faded papered walls
up to the ceiling. My eyes rolled back
in their sockets, counting the nosegays.

Nightmares under the blankets.
Like sodden tufts of moss
bulging virulently green,
mounting the window ledge

and oozing through the open gap,
sooty spores clogging my
nostrils and mouth, the touch
of velvet would make me scream.

I still sleep under those blankets
(their velvet binding rubbed bare)
the self-same ones I pulled around
my shoulders and hid beneath:

now potent and dangerous
as plague-infected blankets thrown
over the walls of a city besieged,
or exchanged for the sacred land

of people with no more immunity
to the pathogens they carried, than I
to the fevers of memory in the folds
and the weave of these old blue blankets.

A Bowl of Apples

A painter looks at a bowl of apples
on a wooden table pushed against
a roughly plastered wall, and sees them
in the same instant as particular
fruits picked from a tree in the garden
or bought at the corner store; noting
yet ignoring the implications
of fading tones and softening forms –
and as abstract ideals of apples.

But whichever I choose, whether
the most elaborate metaphor
or barest statement, words
are too specific. Language
forces definition. Impossible
to write a poem impersonal
as a still-life, or to articulate
the essence of apples, and not
expose my true nature.

My fingers crave the firm touch
of craftsman's tools, pencil, brush,
my nostrils, the reek of size and paint.
I want to understand and feel
through my own flesh the roundness
and bulk of apple pressed against
apple in the bowl's shadowy cradle;
that fierce joy a god must know,
contemplating his work.

What You See

Remember, draw what you see,
you said, not what you think
should be, but what is there.

*

Although the dance of atoms
creates illusions – the picture's
perspectives and solids nothing

more than patterned surface,
metaphoric symbols
for duration and feeling –

yet how to set the scene
and tell the whole story
is not the only problem.

*

A pebble can obscure
the widest view – and you
loom large as Everest.

Almost Immortality

Almost immortality: to be
remembered for centuries
like Azade, slave-girl
of Bahram Gur in Firduz's *Shah Nama* tales

mounted behind, arms tight around his waist
as they hunt gazelles
on a gilt and silver plate

which survived fire and earthquake
warfare and plunder
through the long Sassanid dynasties;
to be admired today by you and me.

A Lost Painting by Balthus

A large blond Siamese cat
with the grave face and stern eyes
of an old Don Juan, stretches full length
along the body of a red-haired girl
on a blue chaise longue, her arms thrown back.

They lie as close as the two sides,
fur and skin, of a smooth sable pelt,
two slices cut from the same apple, or
the tender, perfumed, overlapping disks
of 'Gloire de Dijon' rose petals.

Lovely Hands

'...a terrible thing, to fall
into the hands of a living god.' A fierce hound
bounded toward me. I was the quarry.
The phrase thrummed through my head.

A terrible thing, to fall into such hands.
I knew the god must be Apollo
and the hands not his but those of Marsyas,

darkly varnished by his own blood,
twisting in pain as his skin is flayed, and
the dog the little one in Titian's painting,
lapping the drips congealed below the head
of the challenger, strung upside-down from a tree,

who lost his contest with the master of poetry:
the god who sits on the ground, eyes raised
to the sky, mouth open to sing his triumph,
strumming his golden lyre with lovely hands.

Fingernails

As a girl, I bit my nails to the quick.
Through my twenties, to feel their tips beyond
the ends of my fingers was maddening.
Now, my nails resemble those opalescent,
polished, women's nails which decades ago
were elegant ideals I could no more
imagine on my own fingers than
the silver-sheathed and tallow-coloured
five-inch fingernails of Chinese mandarins.

When I am really old, desensitised
by age and time, I will never cut my nails,
but let them grow until they terrify
whoever looks – wilfully determined
to pre-empt Death's worst indignities;
let them overwhelm our minds with visions
of cemeteries, bodies disinterred from
open coffins crammed with matted hanks
of hair and fingernails like horny spirals.

Never Again

Old age means not being able
to bite into an apple
walk the length of a valley
see every detail in a pattern
hear the highest alto deepest bass
or wrap my legs around your waist.

The Nest

Watering tubs of box and pots of herbs,
one early summer afternoon, I was startled
by an agitated fluttering under
the slatted lower shelf of the wooden table
in the corner of my terrace. Unexpected,
a pigeon (one of the millions of London birds),
scrambled upwards in a flash of grey and white
to fix carnelian eyes upon me and circle
the narrow radius between neighbouring buildings,
but when I went inside, returned at once.

Next time, I stooped to peer under the table
and found the hidden nest. Huddled, silent,
she was brooding her clutch of eggs: two of them,
glowing with potential life, like oval
sections of a perfect arm or breast
from an archaic marble statue. She must
have scavenged every twig and scrap of weed
from nearby gardens. Our gazes met; I knew
she would not budge, now I'd seen her eggs –
would rather die than leave them unprotected.

Late September, I see a pigeon strut
across the terrace tiles on puce-pink feet.
Everything about this bird is fresh and
young and bright – the clean white tail-feathers,
the neon-vivid green and purple ruff
around its neck. Another lands; they bicker like
adolescent siblings, heads darting serpentine.
No sign of the mother – the nest is derelict.
But now it's spring, and here she comes again –
with sappy grass-strands trailing from her beak.

Those Short Seasons

The grim industriousness of trees:
spring leaf and blossom, midsummer
fruit, autumn seed,
all to be produced in a few months –
                         those short seasons.

Crocuses

Pale, bare, tender stems rising
from the muddy winter-faded grass,

shivering petals the almost luminous
blue and mauve of bruises on the naked

bodies of men, women, children
herded into a forest clearing

before the shouted order, crack of gunfire,
final screams and prayers and moans.

Memorials

(for FM, RN & MD)

The tall plant my friend brought from France
still stands in its glazed pot on the steps
by the front door of the house where she used to live
and flowers every summer,

the worn brass candlestick on the kitchen
shelf was my grandmother's (whom I only know
from sepia photographs), that simple object
is her memorial – and

like a bright flower in the wind, the small boy
sways his head as his father's friends play
the tunes, sing the songs, recite the poems
he wrote, praising existence.

A New Book

Cutting the pages of a new book –
the first touch and smell of paper
matt and dense as chamois leather,
the balanced ivory shaft and fine steel
blade of the knife between my fingers.

The feel of the top is rough, pages
half-attached by nubs like knotted
threads in shantung silk. Sometimes
the knife jags and tears a tiny notch
I try to heal with a palm-caress,

then the blade slips smoothly along
the folded edge where two pages join.
Gentle, the pressure of my hand
to flatten and hold them apart. Such pleasure
from your book – before I read a word.

Mosaic

Writing a poem, shifting
words from there to here
is like choosing between
hexagons of tile
for a mosaic, or the next
move in a game of chess.

The final image is clear
in my mind – now abstract
as the Alhambra, then
complex as Ravenna –
kaleidoscope,
jewelled tiara.

But which piece goes
where, which words cohere,
unknowable until
the riddle's solved, the circle
closed, the pattern fixed –
the poem exact.

Deletion

In less than an instant, I can delete dozens
of messages from my computer screen,
watch them vanish as a swarm of mayflies
spirals upward through the hawthorn blossom
in its dance of nuptial suicide,
or iron filings rush towards a magnet.

But those hundreds of words, read then deleted,
do not disappear. The air I breathe
is clogged with them, like pollen in hay-fever season
or prayer that cannot force the heavenly barrier,
the Heaviside layer, to achieve response.
I can imagine them, twisted around each other
like a heavy ball of rubber bands, or
a weightless pale cocoon sheathing the future.

Powder Mountain

What I imagine
as I hear the river ripple
and stare across the flatlands
toward the horizon

is a mountain range
like a master calligrapher's brush-stroke
marking the line
between shadowed earth and glowing sky

each receding ridge dissolving
into gauze veils
mauve   taupe   grey   beige
as evening falls

to know that behind the furthest crest
lie unseen valleys
brimming with emptiness
where the last slant rays

of setting sun
draw back from rock-strewn slopes
and sift down from the peaks
gentle as powdered talc.

Sinking

I was slowly sinking
through a thousand layers,
through darkening washes
of melting topaz-coloured crystals
like onion skins and fish bones
seethed for hours, as slowly
as an aspic thickens;

all that moonless night,
through a thousand layers
of phosphorescent algae-skeins
and hazy plankton colonies,
sinking into darkness
below the deepest currents,
waiting for sleep.

The Fourth Dimension

A slow heave of time, a rupture in space
– like a cold tide accepting a flung stone –
closed over her head. She was lost, gone,
might never have existed.

What difference would it make – even
in the shortish run – if she succeeded?
Stones were hurled, tides rolled in and out,
Space and Time embraced.

The Pool-hall Theory

What happened demonstrates
the pool-hall theory of human nature:
smooth bright shiny coloured balls
banging into each other, then bouncing
off toward the next encounter,
surfaces so hard, nothing
can permeate or be exchanged:
no message, no memory, not an atom.

What at first seemed merely a nudge
across a field of green baize
(like the sheared lawn of a cemetery)
was the perfect move to eliminate
all contenders. But what set them
on course remains mysterious
as explanations of the universe –
or love, trust and forgiveness.

The Jester's Legs

In a field across the valley
the furrows narrow and widen, fold
into each other and vanish – parti-
coloured stripes of green and tan,
earth and crop: the plain and purl
of a jester's fully-fashioned
knitted stockings. And above it,
a row of poplars rustles, shimmers
pales and darkens against the skyline
as every leaf is turned by the wind:
the rapt gaze of an audience
mystified yet captivated
by the chorus-girlish movement
of the jester's prancing legs.

                    And then,
as if an army of hungry
invaders, arrive the harvesters.

Robbery

In the attic of the convent
they found the stockings: fully-fashioned
pale cotton, elaborately
patterned between ankle and calf,
both heels and one toe
meticulously darned, hidden
long ago by some nostalgic
sentimental postulant.

Now imagine two nuns –
a flash of black and white, like magpies
rising from a bare-branched copse –
their high excited voices, the vow
of silence broken
                    by the first lapse
from what they thought forever promised:
mastered by such temptation that
they spent the rest of their lives debating
whether they were robbers –
and how this sin might be atoned.

A Border Incident

Gleaning olives, hard and black as droppings,
green as lizards, leathery or sodden,
where they lay hidden under faded grass
or lodged between the roots of thorny bushes
on the stony ground –
an old Provençal peasant woman, gaunt-faced
as a gypsy sibyl, with sun-stained skin
and work-warped hands, clutched
her back, straightened up, smiled a greeting.

Ignorant, I fantasised
this border territory as archaic,
classical – and wishing I could answer
in Etruscan or Roman Latin, muttered
'Buon giorno'.
I still recall that look of furious insult
as her gap-toothed mouth spat out, 'Bonjour'.
Lucky not to start a local war! (I wonder
if, in forty years, I've learned much more.)

The Anxiety of Airports

Waiting for someone due on a certain plane
and the plane arrives and you strain to scrutinise
every stranger coming through the swinging doors,
wondering if you will recognise him;
your tension increasing, the anxiety level rising;
then only the last few stragglers....
But the person you came to meet does not appear.
(And the explanation, only days later.)

Or flying half-way around the world, a journey of
longueurs and transfers stretched across so many time zones –
wakeful hours in hotel bedrooms and the 4.00 AM call –
until, under flickering neon, adrift along
the static-crackling carpets of inter-terminal
connecting corridors, you're not sure if it's day or night.

And after you've struggled to drag your luggage off
the carousel, negotiated Immigration,
stumbled past the barriers where hotel touts
and drivers holding cards with other people's names
surge forward, and family groups, welcome smiles
set hard, suddenly relax and start to laugh and talk –
the one who should be there for you is nowhere in sight.

So you stand to one side, with the suitcase you're obliged
to guard – though you wouldn't care if it were lost or stolen –
dazed by exhaustion, while the Arrivals board goes blank
and this part of the airport empties of staff and passengers
like water draining down a grating, leaving
only twists of silver paper from candy wrappers,
adhesive shreds of clingfoil like sloughed snakeskins,
and mysterious lengths of white and orange plastic twine.

This is more than childhood fear, this is far worse:
an infant's pre-birth terror of falling through space,
endless abandonment or random malice. But
you force yourself to move, join the queue for a cab,
give the driver an address (though it doesn't sound
right); then sit as far back as you can and
stare out at waterlogged fields and grey suburbs,
uncertain what to expect when you get there.

Plans

The Aymara people of the high Andes believe that the future is hidden, unknown and mysterious, as impossible to see as the skin in the middle of my back, no matter how I turn and twist. They cannot feel regret or disappointment, because they do not make plans.

But the past is unalterable: a coloured map spread across the floor or a landscape seen from a plane, the chance-discovered photograph of what at first seems just a group of strangers, between the pages of a book, then the thrill to recognise the family face; a phalanx of memories, actions and their consequences, sounds and images manifesting before me, to be contemplated – if I dare to look.

When I stare at the sky on a clear night, I must remember that this radiance has its source sometimes as far away as the edges of the universe – has passed through vastnesses of space and aeons of time (as I have been taught to name such things).

Perhaps no one will be left on earth to see the light the furthest stars now emit. As the past exists in the present, and the future's latent image on the present's silvered surface is only revealed, like film in developer, by being lived, I almost understand (and admire, and wish I could emulate) the Aymaras' lack of surprise when things do not turn out as they expect.

An Ichneumon Wasp

No tunes in the head, no music of word or phrase. Inspiration dead. Abandonment. And repeating the story, crooning it like a murderous lullaby, confirms the process, intensifies the damage. Even to think such thoughts is dangerous. To write them, worse.

Or imagine this as possession, not emptiness: an ichneumon wasp lays its eggs inside the pulpy larva of a moth or butterfly. The egg hatches, the creature burrows and gnaws through the living food-source like a cancer consuming inner organs, or dementia ravaging brain cells. Then, its host absorbed, transubstantiated to another form, the new life emerges.

But this metaphor for the amoral balance between destruction and creation is still off-centre, far too simple; does not justify such energetic malice and ordinary misery, nor explain the force that controls you and why you allow it to triumph.

Doom of Kings

Sunset, slow glimmering twilight, then night. We must be driving along the coast road because, moving from left to right across the picture frame, like those cowboy or war movies where the "good guys" always arrive from the left, we pass a signpost pointing down a track to the ferry for the Northern islands.

Sooty red brick walls to each side and arching above, garishly streaked by yellow beams of light, as if overhead lamps were swaying in a strong wind, leaving whole sections in darkness: the palette of a Beckmann painting. A woman selling tickets in the foyer of an old-fashioned cinema might be a priestess at the entrance to her temple. We ask her the way to *Doom of Kings*. She says we have already passed the turning. I vaguely recall, among a list of other place-names on a road-sign, the words *Doom of Kings*, but so faded and insignificant I thought I'd misread it.

I tell him to leave me in the car and go back alone to find the turning – fourth on the right, the cashier-woman had said, but he insists it will be safer to stay together. We set out on foot, right to left, the direction of defeat and failure, and enter a zone of what seem the ruins of 19th-century industrial structures or bombed buildings. Perhaps we are near enough to walk there, though whether 'there' signifies the point the fourth road starts, or *Doom of Kings* itself – whatever the phrase means – remains unclear.

Doom of Kings: that far, northern, edge-of-the-land, end-of-the-world place; its craters and valleys, its dark colours, its frisson of danger; its lure of wisdom and transformation.

A Postcard from Tunisia

Although the scale of the image is too small to see the fine powdery dust lying thick on the panels' curved edges, I can feel its silky texture between my fingers, smell and taste it in the current of air which rises whenever the door is opened or shut. I can sense the exact temperature of the spring sun on the dry paint, note the first signs of flaking.

A few steps back and I am on the street. Sunlight slants from right to left down the alley where, head pensively bowed, like the prince with his enchanted friend in a fairy-tale, a young man leads a sheep (half-turned enquiringly toward him) perhaps to be slaughtered – which might be why he doesn't seem to notice its gaze. The shadow of something or someone out of sight stops just at their feet. High on the wall behind, near a roughly blocked-up door, hangs a black-rimmed, white enamel sign reading Rue Boughedir in Latin letters and Arab script. The narrow colour range: a palette of white, grey, green, ochre, and buff, links its plastered stone – stained by rain-splashed earth where it meets the pale rock-strewn ground – to the greasy matted coat of the sheep and the man's dark jacket.

The cross-lane turns a corner, and half way along stand two flimsy yellow chairs, as if outside a café. Just visible on the road behind, in a tiny space no larger than the young man's shirt, are the bright white façade of a house, and a prayer rug hanging from the balcony railing of a shuttered window.

An obliquely angled house-front, faced by small putty-coloured tiles with an elaborate arabesque pattern pressed into their surface, occupies more than a third of the foreground. Its façade is broken by a large wooden double entrance door rising from the bottom to the top of the card. It could be the door of one of the houses around the Mediterranean where I spent years of my youth. Every detail of its appearance is absolutely familiar: the faded chalky green paint pale as lichen, the four squares of the lower panels like the sides of a dice, the horizontal lozenge above them, and the two narrow panels taller than my height, topped by another lozenge. The brass keyhole cylinder is exactly placed between the lower and upper panels, and the two leaves are divided into eight sections: that endless repetition of the number eight, curved back on itself, which signifies eternity.

Fabulous Beings

Hard not to think of the Atlantic
and the Mediterranean as two
fabulous beings, sometimes warring,
sometimes at peace. So many myths
and stories record their encounters
at Tangier, Tarifa, Gibraltar...

But for me, the meeting of those waters
is signified not by flags or statues
but leaking boats crowded with people
desperate to reach the final border
before being caught by a high-speed
police launch, or drowned in a storm...

What they dream: welcome somewhere
north of the Mediterranean,
far from the Atlantic, is unlikely
to happen. Those fabulous beings
who control their future rarely grant
good fortune – indifferent as the ocean.

The Garden of Eden
(4 February 2003)

It started here, somewhere between
Euphrates and Tigris: the Garden of Eden
where good and evil were first defined.

Now, that appointment with Death
whether in Babylon, Nineveh or
Samarra, seems unavoidable.

*

At the historic sites, shadowed
by half-eroded ziggurats,
hidden aircraft stand prepared

for battles which the six-thousand-year-
old walls of Nebuchadnezar's
imperial city will not survive.

*

The leaders talk of culture-clash.
But all cultures might end here,
where they began – among scattered
body parts and shattered idols.

War Moon

(early morning, 18 March 2003)

It's the night before
spring equinox,
the last day
perhaps, of peace –
and I'm wide awake.

The darkest blind,
heaviest drape,
cannot block out
that brassy glare
bounced back off
the hard stone sphere

of a livid moon
orbiting
our unhappy,
angry world
like a fully armoured
squat, malicious
god of war.

I remember now –
there are languages
where the word for moon
is masculine.

The Threshold

Nineteen eleven, New York City,
the Triangle Shirtwaist Company fire.
A young clerk broke the locked window
of the top workroom, then helped
the sewing girls trapped inside
onto and over the ledge,
launching them into empty space
with a courtly gesture –
as if handing them up to a coach
or introducing them, one by one,
to the most important person
at a grand ball.
A tall girl hugged and gave him a kiss.
When the room was empty, he followed.
From the street the crowd watched.
A better end than
to suffocate in a burning loft.

New York, two thousand and one.
An ordinary autumn morning.
Who were those couples
hurtling past the grid
of innumerable windows
down the façade of the World Trade
Buildings, grasping strangers' hands?
Flames, explosions, the slow
thickening and curdling of smoke;
day after day, the same images;
day after day, one of millions,
I watched them on the television
but dared not violate,
even in imagination,
the final words and gestures
as they helped each other
across the threshold.

TRANSLATIONS

CÉSAR VALLEJO

The Eternal Dice

My God, it makes me cry, the way I live;
it gets me down, having to take your bread;
but this poor, thinking piece of clay
is not just a scab that rose on your side:
your Marias don't leave you.

My God, if you'd ever been a man,
today you'd know how to be God;
but you've always had it so easy,
you don't feel anything for your creation.
The man who puts up with you, he's the God!

Today I am a sorcerer, my eyes lit up
like those of a condemned man,
so God, light all your own candles,
we'll play with the eternal dice...
And maybe, you old gambler, when you stake
the whole universe,
the empty sockets of Death will turn up
like two funereal, slimy aces.

My God, in this dark, stifled night
already your game is over. The Earth
is a flawed dice, worn down
by the spinning of chance;
it can't stop rolling
into the void of an enormous grave.

The Muleteers

Mule driver, fabulously glazed with sweat,
the Menocucho ranch
demands its daily thousand pains to pay for life.
It's noon. We are at day's girdle.
The sun hurts.

Driver, you move in your red poncho
savouring the Peruvian legends of chewed coca.
And I from a hammock,
from a century of doubt,
carp at your horizon and sad surmises,
the mosquitos and the genteel, sickly
refrain of a 'paca-paca'.

At last you will arrive where you are going
driver, who, behind your sly donkey,
depart...
depart...

I wish you well, in this heat where every anxiety
and every reason rear stubborn on hind legs;
when the spirit barely animates the body,
and without coca, you cannot manage
to lead your beast towards the Andes
west of this eternity.

The Spider

It is an enormous motionless spider
colourless, but whose body,
head and a belly, are bloody.

Today I watched her closely. With what effort
she splayed from weary flanks
her many legs.

I brooded on her hidden eyes,
deadly pilots of the spider.

It is a spider who shudders
stranded on a crest of stone;
belly on one side,
head on the other.

Poor wretch, in spite of all her legs
she can't decide. To see that wanderer
dazed by such a blow
has made my whole day bitter.

It is an enormous spider, whose belly
will not obey her head.
I have brooded on her eyes
and on her many legs...
How bitter that wanderer has left me.

Trilce 11

      Time   Time
Midday blocked between night dews.
Bored barrack light-bulb shrinks
time   season   tempo   time
      Era   Era

Crowing cocks scrape the earth in vain.
The mouth of daylight conjugates
era   being   epoch   era
     Tomorrow   Tomorrow

Hot sleep still to be.
The present plans to save me for
tomorrow   future   soon   tomorrow
     Name   Name

What is it called that so hurts us?
It's called TheSame which suffers
name   word   noun   NamE.

Trilce 45

The sea disinherits me
with its moving waters.

We should always be leaving. We should savour
that splendid song, song murmured
by the under-lips of longing.
O prodigious virginity.
A saltless breeze is rising.

From far away I snuff the sap of trees,
hearing the improvisations of the undertow
as it hunts out its notes.

And if thus the absurd
stinks in our nostrils,
we can gird ourselves with the gold of the dispossessed,
and bring to life the unborn wing
of night, sister
of that orphaned wing of day,
who, being alone, still cannot fly.

Mass

The battle ended,
the soldier dead, a man approached
and said, 'Don't die, I love you so!'
But oh, the corpse kept dying.

Two moved close and repeated,
'Don't leave us! Be brave! Come back to life!'
But oh, the corpse kept dying.

Then twenty, a hundred, a thousand, five hundred thousand,
wailing, 'So much love, yet powerless against death!'
But oh, the corpse kept dying.

Millions of people gathered around him
with a common plea, 'Stay with us, brother!'
But oh, the corpse kept dying.

Then all the men on earth stood there;
the corpse gazed back sadly, touched at last;
slowly sat up, embraced the first man
and hurried off...

Black Stone on a White Stone

I shall die in Paris in a rainstorm
on a day I already remember.
I'll die in Paris – I won't avoid it –
perhaps one Thursday, like today, in autumn.

Thursday it will be, because today, Thursday,
writing these lines, I have set my shoulder
against evil; today, as never before, turned
back down my road to see myself alone.

César Vallejo is dead, they all
beat him although he never hurt them;
they gave it to him hard

with club and rope. His witnesses are
Thursdays, the bruised bones of his shoulder,
solitude, rain, roads...

SOPHIA DE MELLO BREYNER

Cyclades

(invoking Fernando Pessoa)

The frontal clarity of this place imposes your presence
Your name emerges as if the negative
Of what you were develops here

You lived in reverse
Incessant traveller of the inverse
Exempt from yourself
Widower of yourself
Lisbon your stage-set
You were the tenant of a rented room above a dairy
Competent clerk in a business firm
Ironic delicate polite frequenter of the Old Town bars
Judicious visionary of cafés facing the Tagus

(Where still in the marble-topped tables
We seek the cold trace of your hands
– Their imperceptible fingering)

Dismembered by the furies of that non-life
Marginal to yourself to others and to life
You kept all your notebooks up to date
With meticulous exactitude drew the maps
Of the multiple navigations of your absence –

What never was and what you never were stays said
Like an island rising up windward
With plumb-line compass astrolabe and sounding-lead
You determined the measure of exile

You were born later
Others had found the truth
The sea-route to India already was discovered
Nothing was left of the gods
But their uncertain passage
Through the murmur and smell of those landscapes

And you had many faces
So that being no one you could say everything

And yet obstinately I invoke – O divided one –
The instant that might unite you
And celebrate your arrival at the islands you never reached

These are the archipelagos that float across your face
The swift dolphins of joy
The gods did not grant nor you wanted

This is the place where the flesh of statues like trembling willows
Pierced by light's breathing
Shines with matter's blue breath
On beaches where mirrors turn towards the sea

Here the enigma that always puzzled me
Is more naked and vehement therefore I implore:

'Why were your movements broken
Who encircled you by walls and chasms
Who spilt your secrets onto the ground?'

Invoke you as though you arrived in this boat
And it were your feet stepping onto the islands
Whose excessive overwhelming nearness
Was like a loved face bending too close

In the summer of this place I call you
Who hibernated your life like an animal through the harsh season
Who needed to be distant like someone standing back to see the
          picture better
And willed the distance he suffered
I call you – I gather the pieces the ruins the fragments –

Because the world cracked like a quarry
And capitals and arms columns shattered to splinters
Heave from the ground
And only a scattering of potsherds is left of the amphora
Before which the gods become foreigners

Yet here the wheat-coloured goddesses
Raise the long harp of their fingers
To charm the blue sun where I invoke you
And invoke the impersonal word of your absence

If only this festive moment could break your mourning
O self-elected widower
And if being and to be would coincide
In the one marriage

As if your boat were waiting in Thasos
As if Penelope
In her high chamber
Were weaving you into her hair

The Small Square

My life had taken the form of a small square
That autumn when your death was being meticulously organised
I clung to the square because you loved
The humble and nostalgic humanity of small shops
Where shopkeepers fold and unfold ribbons and cloth
I tried to become you because you were going to die
And all my life there would cease to be mine
I tried to smile as you smiled
At the newspaper seller at the tobacco seller
At the woman without legs who sold violets
I asked the woman without legs to pray for you
I lit candles at all the altars
Of the churches standing in the corners of that square
Hardly had I opened my eyes when I saw and read
The vocation for eternity written on your face
I summoned up the streets places people
Who were the witnesses of your face
So they would call you so they would unweave
The tissue that death was binding around you

Muse

Muse teach me the song
Revered and primordial
The song for everyone
Believed by all

Muse teach me the song
The true brother of each thing
Incendiary of the night
And evening's secret

Muse teach me the song
That takes me home
Without delay or haste
Changed to plant or stone

Or changed into the wall
Of the first house
Or become the murmur
Of sea all around

(I remember the floor
Of well-scrubbed planks
Its soapy smell
Keeps coming back)

Muse teach me the song
Of the sea's breath
Heaving with brilliants
Muse teach me the song
Of the white room
And the square window

So I can say
How evening there
Touched door and table
Cup and mirror
How it embraced

Because time pierces
Time divides
And time thwarts
Tears me alive
From the walls and floor
Of the first house

Muse teach me the sing
Revered and primordial
To fix the brilliance
Of the polished morning

That rested its fingers
Gently on the dunes
And whitewashed the walls
Of those simple rooms

Muse teach me the sing
That chokes my throat

In the Poem

To bring the picture the wall the wind
The flower the glass the shine on wood
And the cold chaste clearness of water
To the clean severe world of the poem

To save from death decay and ruin
The actual moment of vision and surprise
And keep in the real world
The real gesture of a hand touching the table.

Writing

In Palazzo Mocenigo where he lived alone
Lord Byron used every grand room
To watch solitude mirror by mirror
And the beauty of doors no one passed through

He heard the marine murmurs of silence
The lost echoes of steps in far corridors
He loved the smooth shine on polished floors
Shadows unrolling under high ceilings
And though he sat in just one chair
Was glad to see the other chairs were empty

Of course no one needs so much space to live
But writing insists on solitudes and deserts
Things to look at as if seeing something else

We can imagine him seated at his table
Imagine the full long throat
The open white shirt
The white paper the spidery writing
And the light of a candle – as in certain paintings –
Focussing all attention

MARIA NEGRONI

Three poems from *DHIKR* (1997)

1

The hunter does not expect treachery – his thoughts are simple – .
He trusts in the light which lies with the darkness. With me he
would make the impossible journey (crossing my tracks, following
in my footsteps) towards what I have forgotten and lost. To the
centre of my last demarcation.

The hunter loves me like a blind warrior. After the defeat, he goes
on firing arrows at the night's heart.

2

That woman with a balcony in the hand, with a beach in the balcony,
with an interminable sea in the beach – and so forth. The universe,
in infinite regression, is a private desire. It carries anxiety into my
centre, from where my emotion expels it as a contribution to the
small euphorias of silence.

3

Dusk in the city. A bird in the undulating body of space. The red-
robed bride was crying.

I might have been able to say: I too feel the dusk in my mouth. Or
my song is dreaming it all: red bird, undulating bride, sobbing city.

Bodies inopportunely loved. Eternal regression towards your name-
lessness, my language.

To close the eyes like one who adjusts to uncertainty: Ithaca ship-
wrecked. The scar can be the whole sky.

Three poems from *Night Journey* (1994)

Dialogue with Gabriel III

I keep coming back to the point of departure, the sacristy of a church or a baptistery, in my hotel room in Milan. At once the flight begins again, I and a flock of pelicans. First, a castle and night walls. The shadow of the birds. Only at the end, a well down which I start to fall until I can make out a date in yellow: 1500 and something. I hear myself emit a low cry, almost voiceless, like that of someone who does not know how, or perhaps does not wish, to ask for help. Then everything changes. I feel the touch of cold arms. It is Gabriel, who says: – It is a dream. Stay a while and it will be all right. You have only seen the depth of shadow, the remains from the destruction of something. A shipwreck of the soul. It will pass. My heart calmed, though only for an instant. And if Gabriel were to be trapped, in the dream mirrors? The clearness with which I hear her retreat toward the window and disappear is frightening. Under my body now, the bed feels like tile. From my left side, cramped, gone totally dead, spurts a light and then a fountain and the water gushes violently, everything in the room is confused, I can't find the bell to ask for help from the reception desk but at this the wind starts to blow and carry every object away. The wind and its purpose. I was flying in the inscrutable wind.

Threads of Being

In a Nordic country, Sweden perhaps, she and I (I being both) arrive at the house of a man we used to love. We come to ask him for another chance. The man takes us into his living room. People come and go, wearing fur coats, like turgid shadows in someone's memory. A cold of funerals and mirrors. A cold that knots itself into a country. About midday, we go out for a stroll, and nearby, at sea level, I see a port and derricks and tepid white houses against a stupefyingly blue sky. I say: Istanbul and, at that moment, a piercing desire to cross the border and enter the golden city, the city of the three seas and towers over the Bosphorus...but I didn't bring my passport. When we return, it is already dark. The man, who is a writer, is drinking a magic potion. What does he protect himself from? I drink it also, careful not to think too much, to avoid his eyes, beautiful as being orphaned. Tonight we'll suffocate ourselves in sleep almost to the point of death. We shall not repeat the mistake.

The Book of Beings

As ever, the taxi driver takes me where I do not want to go. Once he lost me in Syria Street, another time in Retiro, four blocks from my mother's house, (when where I wanted to be was the Discoteque Roxy, in Manhattan). Now he has just said that he will leave me in Tetropolis. But this time I do not protest. I just feel a little sad, not knowing that it would have been the same if he had taken me where I wanted to go (that is, if such a place exists). On the radio I hear a strange music, and politely ask what it is. The driver seems offended. – That is not music, they are reciting the Koran. He leaves me in a luminous and empty city, without doors or alphabets or cemeteries. A city of silence, insomniac, between daybreak and Thuringia. – You must know – says the taxi driver – that the only book that matters has already been written and is sung without music and is the most difficult and untranslatable music that exists, – like the pangs of death.

ELSA CROSS

Cantharides

1
The red stone
        – blood of the serpent –
fades into day

light falls on the sanctuary

2
Among the ruins
dry cantharides
glinting husks
scald–scabs

traces of aloe
on the tongue

3
Serpent
        the one who knows and begets
        who conceals
        annihilates

to reach her
you must become a wind
penetrate rock fissures

be the fire's tongue
        arrow of the god

4
Where they broke
the holy amphorae
she hides herself

her words
     scattered stones

between muffled footsteps
and thorns
her fractured song

   5

In her agile spirals
her green suffocations
her pleated silks
I breathe

I let the dust adhere to my ribs
the wind hiss between my teeth

in her Orphic circles
her geometric eyes
her serpentine embrace
I expire

   6

Word
dry blood on the rock
     threads of a voice

palpitate on the tongue
approach and retreat
     explode
in a naked blaze

semen and light

   7

Intermittent
     blows of a voice
combine and rear up
into a single silence

     – hurricane eye

8

Resonance the stones enclose

the echo
         tumbles
         like a landslide

tangles of buzzing bees

                  twitched threads

9

The shrill sound
hangs in the air
becomes a bellow
               bull-roarer
penetrates pavilion
               labyrinth –

a multicoloured vector.

10

From the open mouth
               as from a mask
syllables cascade
               a gush of sound –

eye of silence

11

Words knot the form
in their mesh

honeycomb
               humming

the dream of the nymphs
nourished by their sap

12

Stuttering tongue
ripples
          of syllables

tongue of fire

devoured by its own phrases

13

From her mouth to my ear
words

the web tears
what grasped now flows
toward the west's burn

14

It hums between the chinks

slides soft fingers along the neck
briefly touches the thigh

it is the sure needle
sharp whistle   arrow

15

It passes through strata
               of meaning
that humid sentence

          wine filtered from
               a closed pitcher

16

In exchange for one flower
          of immortality
among the tense nettles
she leaves the skin
         as pledge

the wind bevels
         her scales

17

And the thorny voice
holds in its dry sheath
an empty shape

curls on the tongue
         like a living word
circles the haunch
like a sibilant hiss
         like a flame

18

She unfurls her coils
rears up
         from the dust
friend of those who imitate
         her cadences

her new skin shines
         – oh Radiant One
a sure target for your arrows

19

She seeks out the angle
where the ray of sunlight
touches the eye's surface
and plays at reflection

her shackled tongue sleeps
feigns that it sleeps
stretches into its fullness
savours its own darkness

20

She casts an invisible snare
like a scent

curls into a circle
lets her echoes fall
to the crevice's depths

21

In tatters
        the careful weft
nothing left in the hands
fragments of sense
                skin-scraps

22

She enters the darkness

unborn words
between these rocks

23

Voice
        contained in the air
word
        suspended in voice
        – and the word, from where?

they have already forgotten

24

It disappears
        into the light's centre

silence devours the words
like tiny insects
                cantharides

VICTOR MANUEL MENDIOLA

Your Hand, My Mouth

1. A plate is a hand hollowing with thirst or hunger.

2. A plate is a hand opening its depths to receive or to grasp.

3. Although its kindly aspect gives me hope, the plate – this hand – has no qualms.

4. The plate gives, shams generosity, but the knife is close behind.

5. The plate is a hard and dreadful hollow. In spite of its measured and pleasant appearance, blood and bones lie at the bottom.

6. It does not matter if I am well or badly dressed, it does not matter if I am well or badly behaved, when the plate rests before me, it overpowers me and makes me – whether I become boy or woman – the armed man.

7. A plate on the table is a moon over a ghastly wood.

8. On the hard plane
   of the wooden table
   unmoving, bleeding,
   the moon's plate.

9. A cup is a hollow which cannot decide whether to open or close, to reveal itself or to hide.

10. The cup gambles, balancing between two waters or two continents at the same time. It is pretty, but a liar.

11. A glass is a fearsome hollow; frightened to lose its contents.

12. A glass stretches upward, apprehensive.

13. With its insolent aspect, the glass assumes a false arrogance.

14. If the glass lets itself be carried away by fear or self-importance, it closes, becomes a bottle; a scar rises like a knot. A navel.

15. When a glass totters, who knows the reason why my life oscillates, filled with astonishment.

16. In the narrow neck of the bottle – like a shut purse, a sealed sex – are neither words nor fellow-feeling in common. There is a measure to guard, a pip or seed to keep hidden. The glass seals itself not only for protection. It doesn't want to share, unless they pay the price.

17. When a plate breaks something essential collapses. Love or the family. Whatever promise or pact. Whatever embrace. Even the kiss withers. It knows the worst.

18. To be startled or frightened: to have eyes as wide as plates.

19. On the surface of a plate I can see the sky of my house or of the world. The Tao begins in a plate or in the hand. Then comes the balcony.

20. On the surface of a plate I can find, in white shadow, your face.

21. There is a white shadow on the plate, a pale shadow in the polished depth. A phantom that watches me every day from the glaze.

22. In the measured hollow of a plate are your hollows, the centimetres of your bite, the hidden hour of digestion.

23. Close to the plate, the knife praises the toothed gum.

24. Close to the plate, the fork stays silent, devious and alert, like the devil's gaze.

25. In its innocuous way, the spoon licks the soup with its little gloomy complicit face.

26. In its round expanse, the plate observes you; draws you into it.

27. The plate has the blindness of eyes glazed white. You were the needle of its gaze aimed at the quarry.

28. A plate is the cloud of smoke from a cannon or the glow a corpse emits. Consider this well.

29. In the centre of the plate you place, naively and gently, the meat of a bull, a pig or a lamb. Do you believe it? Do you imagine that the fierce laws of saliva that poisons or teeth that rend and tear do not apply to you?

30. In the centre of the plate you place the speed of a lettuce. The air blows on the greenness.

31. In the dining-room you listen to the hammer, the shudder, the dread, the drum of the plates.

32. In the centre of the plate see how the zebras unrave into black white fibres. On each plate there is an African motif. The lion is on the prowl.

33. The plate supports the bull, the lamb and the large green leaf, revealed between shriek and canine tooth.

34. The plate appears a surface, but it is the snare of a withdrawn purse. A claw like a bloody gauntlet. A belly.

35. From childhood I saw the white shadow of the plate and yearned to plunge into its muddy lake of blood.

36. The plate is a carnivorous plant.

37. By that plant you measure your hunger and thirst; the weight and length of your step; the kilos of pressure in your bite.

38. To sit down to eat with someone, to be at table, to make a gentle or brutal clatter of plates: to represent the digestion inside in the theatre outside.

39. The sounds from my belly and yours at this moment were our words of love two hours ago in front of our plates.

40. On the surface of the table glistens the mute depth of my plate, its blue sound pierces my mouth.

41. I look at your eyes; I look at you hungrily; I look at you with my mouth. I want to contain you; let me embrace you with my belly.

42. When we say 'I love you' or 'I want you' we do not mean the smile or the hair, much less the shoulder; it would be better to speak as we speak in the silence of the bed or the bath. Feelings make me a liar.

43. In the dominion of the plate I can say: I need to smell your foot, taste your sour unfolding armpit, inhale the grave-pits of your hot neck, touch the ring of your body, eat you, eat from your hollows. Gnaw your bone, your inside. Let me.

44. When we no longer love, then we do not eat together nor eat each other. The theatre of outside displaces the interior theatre. We are not a plate that races at the furious pace of its pleasure but rather a glass tightening itself without accent or rhyme.

45. On a plate you do not only put your food; you place the ounces and inches of your body. Your flesh and your bones. Most of all, your hollows.

46. An equation: desire = hunger, or the opposite; but perhaps this would be far better: love = plate = mouth = belly.

47. The plate is an open mouth. Feed it.

48. Under my nose, in front of my eyes, I watched two snails become two mouths on my plate. It was the most passionate kiss in the history of cinema.

49. I think of you and divide you with the cutlery of my tongue. No need for spoon or fork or knife.

50. The plate is your mouth when you come close to me. I listen to the beads of your little teeth.

51. The plate teaches me your most delicious hollow. That is why I dabble my finger in your dinner.

52. When I kiss your mouth, I kiss your deepest hollow. And I know where it starts and where it ends.

53. It is not your eyes, not your nose, not your ears which have this depth, this emptiness which encloses me and fills me. Your cunning words, your tongue, are my evidence.

54. Give me food from your plate, surrender your internal world, give me your hunger.

55. Now comes my mouth to your plate to eat from your hand.

56. I put half a tomato on the plate's surface: I see in you the insolent crest of a white cock inspecting his domain. Complacently counting the cows and chickens.

57. I place a sprig of dill on my plate; I watch your hand grow over my hand.

58. – I go to the market. I snatch olives from the counter; tear off three branches; move my eyes along the immobile swiftness of a salmon, frozen into the oceanic vessel of sweet ice in the Fish and Seafood department. The spur of a shark, the claws of a crab. I order three pieces.

I return, laden, to my house. A full bag.

On a slow fire, for not more than twenty minutes, I cook my catch.

Prepare it for you. Butter. Two sprigs of dill. You will like it.

Come, nearer, hear this music of blood and fire, eat with me. Come to my house, sit down to eat at my table. Let me enter into you, before I enter you.

59. Your plate is a delicious grave. Bury me.

SOPHOCLES

Jocasta's death
FROM *Oedipus Rex* (LINES 1223-85)

2ND MESSENGER:
  Honoured nobles of this land
  what dreadful thing you are about to hear,
  and see with your minds' eye;
  what great woe will overcome you,
  if you feel kinship to the house of Labdacus!
  Not even the mighty rivers, not Istus nor Phasis,
  could scour this house clean from pollution.
  So much hidden evil exposed,
  will it or no. The worst woes
  seem those we bring upon ourselves.

CHORUS:
  What we know already
  is bad enough. What more will you say?

2ND MESSENGER:
  The shortest tale to tell and to hear –
  our royal lady, Jocasta, is dead.

CHORUS:
  Poor wretched woman – how?

2ND MESSENGER:
  By her own hand.
  But you are spared the worst – you did not see it all.
  I'll tell you, though, what I can drag from my mind –
  where it's already buried –
  of her pitiful end.
                      Frantic, she rushed into her rooms,
  to the marriage chamber, slammed the door behind her,
  and threw herself onto the bed,
  tearing her hair with desperate fingers
  and calling on Laius as if he were not dead
  to remember the night they lay together
  and made the one who would kill him –
  then left her to be a mother to polluted children.

Weeping, she cursed her evil double fate:
to bear a husband from a husband,
and children from her own son.

I cannot tell you more about her death,
for then, Oedipus, roaring with grief,
burst into the hall and I could only watch him,
raging around the walls, begging one after another
to give him a sword – and tell him where
to find it, that double-ploughed field:
his wife, his mother, and mother to his children.
One of the gods must have shown him the way –
it was none of us who were near, we were too frightened.
                    Shouting in frenzy,
he threw himself at the great double doors,
tore the hinges apart, and fell into her room –
and we saw, o horrid spectacle, the woman hanging,
her neck entangled in a noose of coiled rope.

Then, with what a ghastly roar he leapt
to loosen the cord and lay her gently on the ground.
Poor suffering man – and the horror,
to watch him tear away the beaten golden brooches
from each shoulder of her robe, lift them high
and plunge them into the sockets of his eyes,
crying out that they should never see him again,
nor what he suffered nor the evil he did,
nor look on those they should not –
but only darkness, forever.
Like a dirge, over and over he chanted,
lifting the pins, striking through his eyelids
until bloody matter spurted down his cheeks and beard –
not drops, but a gush like black rain
or hail drenching him.

All this was their fated doom,
husband and wife – evils doubled between them.
The old happiness was finished,
but it had been real. Now,
anguish and despair, madness, dishonour and death –
every evil assailed them; no curse forgotten.

Mottoes

If you run with the hare
and hunt with the hounds
you fall between two stools.
No changing horses in mid-stream.
Where you make your bed
you have to lie,
among roses and thorns. Really,
it's like the boy who cried, 'Wolf!'
when he saw a lost dog from the pack.
In the land of the blind
the one-eyed man... so don't try,
we all know how it ends.

A Couple

As smug as death,
Daphne and Dorian Gray,
eternal honeymooners,
plunge into another tango.

To be forever young
seemed the best gift
to ask of the Devil.
Since then, they must have danced
ten times around the world.

Like melting sugar skulls
at a *Todos Santos* picnic
in Mexico City,
or a gallant hussar's
fancy epaulettes,

those perched smiles
above each other's shoulder –
mimicking a lust that bores them.
Mais toujours la politesse.

A Saga

Cold scents the path.
Cold ores salt the caves and cliffs.
Stars sift light
through the black veil night wears,
and the sea nudges against earth's rocky breasts.

On the weed-strewn beach
below the walls of the castle keep
she gathers bands of purple kelp
curled tight as a whip
and watches the horizon change:
Azure. Ultramarine. Indigo.

Beyond that line
where ocean plunges down the edge of the world
and the sky curdles and thickens and follows over,
each yearning to meet the other,
a high-prowed boat with russet sails is moving closer.

Phallic Sapphics

Close your eyes against accordion angles
opening out like ivory fans, poker
hands and velvet theatre curtains, or bivalves
to the swirling tide.

Watch instead a runnel of lime-charged water
slowly drip from a stalactite to pattern
the slick wet sides and floor of a karstland cave
with mineral lace.

Remember the bird you once held on your palm,
how it struggled to fly? Its hot hard feathers
in panic-flutter were striped with the same pale
onyx colours as

shingle under almost invisible waves,
or smooth skin sliding through my practiced fingers.
The bird was blinded by fear. But your eyes blur
in expectation.

Romance

(for Assia)

Every time I fold the laundry
I remember when she told me how
it took an hour to put the clothes away,
and that meant every day.

Eyes flashing, she made the list
of her duties into a metaphor.
She looked like a Minoan goddess, or Yeats'
princess bedded on straw.

She seemed to gloat on oppression,
as if it were the fuel and source
of her obsession, and each passionate protest
a further confirmation.

My spirit shrivelled, like fingers
from harsh soap and cold water,
to hear this version of the same old story.
Yet I could not doubt her.

Fairy-tales are very specific,
almost domestic – tasks to be done,
problems to solve. They tell about bewitched
princesses, toad princes,

and the force that holds them spell-bound.
Smoothing his shirts, she dreamed
of transformation and reward, and being
happy ever after.

I'd gone down that road before,
and knew its forks and sudden twists
where one false step has mortal consequence.
But I was luckier.

Homage

It's not a case of forget or forgive.
Who expects either?
Something different happens.
I haven't forgotten
what you did to me or what I did.
I think about it often.
A steady contemplation
can dissolve the need for action
as acid soil consumes cloth, bone, wood.
After a time, even the metal's gone.
Nor have I forgiven.
Forgiveness would be understanding
why those burials were so elaborate.
To the few surviving rituals
of a lost tradition, I pay homage.

A Mourner

I put my head on my arms on my desk
to weep, and the smell and heat of my breath
remind me of afternoons at school
when the teacher made us stop our noise
and running around, and take a rest.

Not since then, except in love's
embrace, have the damp intensities
of my own body and feelings so
combined. My pain is this particular
odour, this primeval climate.

The teacher talked about an endless
age of fire and flood and earthquake,
everything changing, life-forms dying
and being born. In all the confusion
and turmoil, there should be a mourner.

Until You Read It

Like music on the page
which has to be played
and heard, even if
only by one person,
this word, this phrase,
this poem, does not exist
until you read it.

This Time of Year

Parked cars on the street have pale leaves
plaqued to their roofs and windscreens
after the storm, and the same sodden
mosaic is pressed into the pavement
(the pattern fallen cloth-scraps mark
on a tailor's floor). This time of year
the last leaves on the trees are stained
with the watered colours of Mother's chiffon,
crêpe and sharkskin pre-war frocks.

This time of year, my mnemonic
for the date of Daddy's birthday was:
If the eleventh is Armistice Day,
it's the seventh; an association
hard to detach from such concepts as Father,
and God and birth and death et cetera,
when my father had gone to the war.
Nightly, in the double bed,
Mother and I read *Mother India*
together, enthralled by the gory details,
and tried to imagine him there.

They always happened in November,
several consecutive Novembers
(he must have come home then – Mother's
mouth would soften in remembrance):
our worst battles. To break his hold
and her power. There was much
damage. A normal adolescence.
This time of year, between the dates
of their deaths, with a swirl of brittle leaves,
foggy muslin veils and ice-blue glitter
(does it come too late, that promise?)
the forgotten returns. As if
for some purpose. Stronger than ever.

Lineage

When my eyes were sore or tired or itched,
clenching her hands in a loose fist,
my mother would rub her wedding ring,
carefully, along the closed lids,
sure the touch of gold was curative.

She also believe in hot water
with lemon, first thing in the morning
and, at any time of day, drank awful-
tasting infusions and pot-liquors
to purify her blood. She warmed
a spoonful of sweet almond oil to pour
into my aching ear, wrapped torn
old woollen vests around my throat,
and blistered my chest with a poultice
if I came down with a cold.

Remedies and simples from the old
country, still useful in the city,
were passed from mother to daughter
and not yet scorned. We rarely saw
a doctor. When I was little
it seemed normal to be sickly
for half of the year. I never told her
that I was proud she was a witch.

Nails and Spiders and Jacks

First, four flat-headed shiny tacks
had to be hammered into the top
of an empty wooden spool, after
the last span of thread was unreeled, measured
the full stretch of my mother's arm,
and pushed through the eye of a needle.
Then I'd untangle ends of crochet
skeins and darning wool from her workbox
and take one of her crimped and coppery
hairpins – which was just the right tool
for looping yarn up and over the tacks
and through the bobbin's hollow centre.
As long as I went on making the same
movements (like a spider extruding its silk)
the motley cord kept growing.
Later, I'd coil it into a doily
or a tea-cosy – something I thought
was pretty – to give her for a present.

And there was jacks: a game we played
with small glittering silvery objects –
each like six nails joined together
into a three-dimensional Greek cross,
a dice-chassis, a tank-trap,
or a nervous spider signalling
his mating intentions – that had to be tossed
in the air from the back of the hand and land
on your open palm while trying to catch
a rubber ball before it stopped bouncing.
I almost choked from the excitement.

The jack's six arms had clubbed tips
like the four nails in the wooden bobbin.
Remembering one brings back the other –
a connection that seems more important
than the shape of nails and jacks. Perhaps
it was a diagram of how
a message travelled from deep in the brain
through fibres finer than gossamer silk

until it reached my body's furthest limits.
Those childhood speculations.

Crosses and nails. Sixes and fours.
Trap-door spiders and private pleasures.
The game can be played with stones, shards,
dibs or jacks. Checkstones were buried
in Roman tombs and Celtic barrows,
where primitive looms are also found.
Angels and devils gamble for your soul,
they say, with ball and knucklebones –
and not only if you're Christian.
But I didn't know any of this,
polishing my skill at jacks
or musing over my French knitting.
I might have been thinking, though, about space
and pattern and number, female spiders
eating their husbands, shiny metallic
broad-headed nails and blunt-tipped jacks.

Tosca

Above the walnut cabinet where
Uncle Roscoe kept pistols and bullets,
moulds and targets and tins of pellets,
dust motes drifted through a shaft of sunlight
while my Aunt Ann and I listened
to *Tosca* broadcast from the Met.

I know it was summer, because a layer
of dust below the glittering swirl
dulled the linoleum's pattern, and that meant
the carpets had been stored until winter.

But which pattern was it, which room –
before or after our move –
am I remembering, where we sat
between the radio and the cabinet,
which sunny Saturday afternoon,
during the war, assembles
around me as I listen to *Tosca*
now, in a half-dismantled apartment
the day before a new departure.

I have heard *Tosca* so often,
I think I know each motif
by heart. The grand themes of my life
must have been already waiting
in the wings, incarnated as
the jealous woman artist,
Scarpia's potent menace. Those two
make the couple. Cavaradossi's
revolutionary fervour can
never deflect their trajectory
of mutual destruction.

Uncle Roscoe's guns and bullets
somehow stay connected to the story,
but he was gentle, indifferent
to the passions of the music –
and the wife he had chosen:

that thwarted fantasist of every
métier and alternative.

So much talent misdirected
into trimming hats and bottling fruit.
She taught me to listen to opera,
to believe I was an artist,
to read Baudelaire and to iron a shirt
as well as a Parisian laundress.

Tosca is telling the whole world
how she has lived only for art, and I
an in another place and apartment,
writing my notes, watching dust motes drift
in the sunlight, about to move on.

Aunt Ann's floral-patterned linoleum
on one or other living-room floor
crumbled decades ago. Each house
was gone when I tried to find it,
the gardens asphalted over.
I never learned what happened to her
walnut cabinet, or Uncle Roscoe's
collection of guns, after they died.

The Fish

Trying to think it through,
force my mind to hold one specific
thought, makes my brain convulse and twist in my
skull like a fish in a net, with a fish's vigour.

I see the fixed glare of its eye – blood,
jet and mica – feel the rasping touch
of fin and scale against my hand, the tail's
last spiny flick and panic-thrust as it
wrenches free; and I am left wondering
what it was I tried to think about, depleted

yet glad that now I can follow it through
                    all the way to the sea.

Visitation

A foam-crimped wave clear and silent
as a sheet of glass slid across
the shingle that wets your feet before
you notice then dulls and vanishes

or a sigh of wind under the door
that lifts the carpet's corner a single
moment and lets it settle as if
nothing happened though you know it did.

The Law

Like someone walking a tightrope
or trying to stay upright
on a heaving platform – first
one foot, then the other,
backward, forward, swaying,
arms stretched shoulder high.

Never before have feet
and fingers felt so alive,
reaching out to sense
the slightest shift in balance
and position, like the growing
tips of trees or vines.

For things to stay the same
they must keep changing.
So the way to change your life
is to be still and do
nothing, while everything else
follows the law of change.

New-born

From the roof of her under-reef den
a giant Pacific octopus –
whose suckered legs are metres long,
who changes tone when curious
from glowing white to glorious red –
hangs a hundred thousand eggs
clumped into strands, like clusters
of grapes painted on the ceiling
of Sennefer's tomb at Luxor.

'The rough surface of rock
makes the vine-tendrils and fruit
more realistic. The artist's
experiment has succeeded...',
the guidebook says. I remember
that tomb in the Valley of the Nobles
more clearly than the others.
An arbour of freshness and coolness
lay below its dusty entrance –
a foretaste of the Western Kingdom.

Sennefer was Mayor of Thebes
and overseer of Amon's
temple garden, three and a half
millenia ago – yet
the vivid colours on the frescoes
and ceiling look newly painted,
the lotus held to his nostril
still fragrant, the grapes luscious.
His wife is young and beautiful.
She tenderly touches his leg
as they stand at the offering table
or sit together, pilgrims
on a boat to Abydos.

The third leg from the right
of a male octopus is modified
with a groove for mating.
When its tip is pushed into

the female's mantle cavity
a long tubular bag of sperm
slides down to find the oviduct.
An octopus is a solitary creature –
this rarely happens more than once.

For the next six months the female
stays in her den, stroking
the clusters of fertilised eggs
with gestures I want to interpret
as consciously gentle, even
maternal, shooting streams of water
from her siphon to keep them free
of fungus and oxygenated.
She will not eat again.

Wasted flesh   skin
peeling like blistered paint
off a ransacked tomb's mildewed walls
or the weightless husks and residue
of grapes pressed dry –
drifting like a grey ghost
trailing mummy bandages
across the ocean floor.
Now the eggs are hatched
her purpose is achieved
if two survive.

A hundred thousand octopus-
existences break through
the membrane web that sheaths them
and float out to the darkness
of the circling current
like souls departing for eternity
or new-born gods.

The Cranes

Far and high overhead, the cranes
were hard to sight but could be heard
the valley's length. Then a plane appeared
to pass through them, and showed them
clear against the racing clouds
and vapour trails in the mild noon sky.

Each bird marked another point
inside an ever-changing space
or on its surface – like the junction knots
in the mesh of a strong net, where
a huge, half-transparent, half-
imagined being, powered by
its own fierce jet and surging thrusts,
was streaming out glory pennants.

We saw new constellations forming
as patterns altered in all dimensions
and trapped the pale print of an almost
full equinoctial moon.
The cranes veered and banked, following
the river's thermals and currents.
We saw cherubim and seraphim
above the Rio Grande.

Late Low Sun

A late low sun
shone through each small new leaf on the vines.
Rows of gnarled brown stocks
pruned for decades to the same height,
and this year's shoots
tethered along the trellis wires,
sprouted new growth –
foliage translucent as lime jelly,
gaudy as stage jewellery

– as if a flock of butterflies
just emerged from their chrysalides
had landed on the vines and spread
tender, crumpled greeny wings
to harden and dry.

Late low sun,
a fluttering in the air. A double-
headed creature
settles on the stony terrace wall.
Pin-eyes fixed
in opposite directions, antennae
at full stretch
and thread-legs braced,
two thin and downy bodies
almost hidden
by dark-veined wings that keep shuddering.

All at once,
still joined, they lift and veer, erratic,
into the branches
of the chestnut tree, whose ruffles of buds
and half-furled leaves,
where sunset's intensest purple rays
strike through,
are the exact colour and shape
to shelter ecstatics.

Flowing Stream

Shadows of leaves
on the pavement I'm laying
with stones from the garrigue
are drifting across it
like clear water in a shallow stream.

Shadows of chestnut
acacia and elder leaves
ripple like water in sunlight
over smooth pale stones
which might be a stream bed.

The movement of shadows
silhouettes of leaves
speckle the cobbles, the wave-worn
limestone slabs of unclassifiable
lichen-spotted shapes

and alter the pattern
by glittering refraction
as the water eddies
around fallen twigs and pebbles
on the sandy stream bed, on the paving

Until I don't know
whether shadows or reflections
wind or stones or leaves
are the transparent water
in a flowing stream.

Thunder

I am very good at chimpanzee's work:
shelling almonds, picking stones out of lentils,
scratching a smear of food off a sleeve or collar.
I find a satisfaction in repetition,
superstition, and know the myopic's refusal
to look above or beyond the horizon. Half
of my nature is simple as a medieval
peasant. The other isn't, and that's the problem.

It's harder to date the complex of discontents
shared by any metaphysical primate,
who soon learns that pain is surer than pleasure.
A stubbed toe hurts, and the soul asserts itself
by the same token. Such thoughts are as timeless
as wondering how the planets started spinning
and why one cannot live forever.
Elegies must be the oldest art form.

Thunder rolls from the northern hills, and the lamp
on my desk flickers. Once, it would have been
an omen, a god's voice or seven-league tread.
Now it's only a nuisance, or a warning
reminder of how easily the world could end.
There are days in the present when I imagine, far
in the future, someone brooding on first and last things,
keening the dead, and tending her garden.

Buds

From late November until the solstice –
what used to seem the lowest notch
before the sky-ratchet nudged forward –
I have begun to notice, on vines
and shrubs and trees I'd thought were dead,
half-hidden below those few
stiff, discoloured leaves that cling
to dull twigs and dry branches, hundreds
of swelling, glossy new buds.

Such confidence and stubbornness
makes one reconsider. Those old leaves
protect next season's growth.
The blackish trunks can still pump,
through months of winter, enough sap
for most buds (their scaly sheath,
their fragile freight of protoplasmic
leaf and pulpy, pleated petal)
to survive, hold on. Once
you know where to look, confirmation's
omnipresent: not a moment's
hiatus between death and life.

Solstice

A door swings open
slow and heavy
on rusty hinges.

A wheel revolves
heavy, jolting
against the fulcrum
of its wooden axle.

A round winter moon
disentangles
from roofs and branches

to float above
snow-blanked fields
and rocky mountain peaks
weightless, easy

on the humming pivot
star-gleam flashing
of the new year solstice.

On the Coast Road

(north of Dubrovnik, 1989)

A mosaic of broken glass (halting the traffic)
strewn across the sun-dappled, heat-softened coast
road surface, fills a larger space than when
it was a windscreen; and the undamaged door
of a new bronze Mercedes makes the crumpled fenders
seem ancient and fragile, like a chariot unearthed.

Two men, with movements as rapid as dancers,
cut into the side of the car and manoeuvre
the pieces apart. Is that sound the whine
of an electric tool slicing through metal
or a faint scream from the trapped driver?
The blue plush bear lolling against a wheel
and the red pantalooned clown appear unhurt,
but there's no sign of a child whose toys they are.

A high terrace overlooks the corner
where the local car smashed into the tourist,
like a box at the theatre. The terrace is crowded
with people pressing against the railings to see
everything better. Their faces are concentrated
but calm, like angels watching the damned suffer.

Chardin's *Jar of Apricots*

The jar is half-full with the soft gleam
of dark gold apricots, and has a sheet
of parchments tied across the top.
Chardin painted it at the same age
we both are, noting the different
transparencies and thicknesses
of wine glass and jar – and the decorated
cup with a spoon inside, pieces of bread,
crumbs and a knife, the orange or lemon
and paper parcel on the wooden table
pushed against a soft taupe wall
in the oval frame. I look at it
for a long time and the painting opens
into another sort of time,
with its own depth and light and meaning,
like a childhood memory. No!
Make it go beyond the old story,
but keep the timelessness of the child's
first concept of eternity –
which might have come while staring through
the reflecting sides of a half full
jar of apricots on the kitchen-table.

EIGHT POEMS FROM

TWELVE SIBYLS

Squatting at the Womb's Mouth

Swaddled in feathers and cloth
a keen old face peers out through
what could be the entrance to a burrow
or a hanging nest

but she is not that sibyl, so shrunken, so ancient
who pleaded for death

her gaze is too cool
with an abbess's shrewdness, an ambassador's
judgement, the tolerance
and wisdom of the Great Mother

squatting at the womb's mouth
giving birth to herself.

Facts About the Sibyl

The total lack of charm Heraclitus stressed,
that she started to utter prophesies
the moment after her birth and drank bull's blood,
are facts about the Sibyl I find of interest.

She put the Golden age far in the future,
not the distant past, and was as hostile
to idolatry as a Hebrew. She refused Apollo
her virginity, and never wore perfume.

She said that when she died she would become
the face in the moon – go round and round like the moon –
released from her oracular ecstasy.
Only a sibyl can outstare the sun.

After Possession

She stands between the bird and silent crowd
with her vulture epaulettes and voodoo hairstyle,

with thick veined hands as stiff and cold as clay
that touch each other, unbelievingly,

and the closed smile of the survivor's perfect
knowledge, total recall. Like a stopped cyclone.

His Face

This place must seem a larger cage to my birds
than it does to me. The dark passage where
questioners wait on shallow benches and
the cavern roofed with arching rocks it leads to,
the hidden alcove and cool cistern, define
our territory. Only at night, sometimes,
when no one will see, I go outside to watch
the birds' black shapes move against the sky
like a loom's shuttles weaving stars and clouds
closer, and read the text they trace, whose fine
calligraphy encodes tomorrow's answers.

Then, with a special sound between a moan
and whistle, I bring them down to settle.
I am cloaked and hooded. The touch of a beak
on my lips is cold as the serpent's tongue licking
my ears when I was a girl in Apollo's temple
and learned the language of birds. What they whisper
has a trickster's glamour, but their night-
patterns between the planets incarnate
the god. For one moment, before the first
beams of the dawn sun pierce that image,
my flock of wheeling birds becomes his face.

Dreamy

Since early this morning
the big blonde sibyl is dreaming
hunched over, clasping her knees,
like a girl at the edge of a field
staring into the tall grass
toward a distant line of trees,
remembering where she came from,
how the look and smell of everything
was different.

One of the temple birds
has settled on her back.
The dusty weight feels comforting.
She senses it is just as mournful
and dreamy as she. The bird
is brooding migration,
a river glinting direction,
hearing again the raucous cries of the flock.

They know they will not leave
this place. They both belong to the god
now, forever.

Inward

Her eyes are staring inward
into a space as endless
as the distance from here to the mountains

she has forgotten. Between
those peaks and this high cave
lies the drowned valley floor where it happened –

whatever gave her the look
of a violated woman
or a bird that clings to a storm-struck mast

and made everything fade –
like being formed from clay and breathed
into life. Or a god's visitation.

Elegant Sibyl

Having become an expert at false tones
as the voices slide lower or higher than intended
out of control, having heard so many lies
seen so many faces altering crazily
trying to hide their real motives,
having pondered the fate of those who came to consult her
and how little difference any words make,
her gaze is now withdrawn and watchful as a diplomat's.
Her lips, though still full, meet firmly in a straight hard line.

But her feathered cloak and tall head-dress of glorious plumage
are so elegant, no one can resist her.
The Emperor comes to hear her pronounce almost daily.
All the rich men's wives copy her style.

Alone at last, she strips off her regalia
lets the fine cloak drop to the floor
pushes strong fingers through the stubble of cropped hair
and climbs into the deep stone bath of water so cold
that even at the height of summer she shudders, and in winter
the effort of will the action demands
has become her greatest indulgence.

Only then is she able to think of the god and wait his pleasure.

The Egg Mother

In the same soothing tone the god uses
before he mounts her, she whispers
secrets that the stars and trees have told her
against the bird's warm neck
then grips him firmly around feathery sides.

His strong wings raise them high above the coast
and follow the river's trail
glinting up the valley to its mountain
source. Brought on the backs
of their oracular birds to a rock-strewn field

below the summit line, sibyls gather:
the Delphic and the Persian,
Cumaean, Erythraean, Tiburtine,
and those from even further –
sudden green oases, weed-fringed islands.

As if it were the Orphic World Egg,
a silver moon floats up
to signal her arrival, and all the women
turn to watch the bird
settle, and catch her first words and smiles.

Using the same tones their gods do,
gentling them into submission,
she strengthens her sisters for their stern duties.
She is the oldest now.
Her time has come to be the Egg Mother.